# Contents

 **Fiction**

**Rivals**
page 2

 **Non-fiction**

**History of cool**
page 14

*Written by*
**Dee Reid**

*Illustrated by*
**Dylan Gibson**

*Series editor* **Dee Reid**

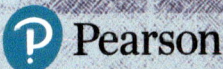

# Characters

Imran

Tariq

The girls

## Tricky words

- mirror
- clothes
- laughed
- really
- other
- giggled

*Read these words to the student. Help them with these words when they appear in the text.*

## Introduction

Tariq is in the year above Imran at school. Sometimes they get on OK but sometimes Tariq likes to boss Imran around. One break time, Imran was in the toilet. He was looking at himself in the mirror. He thought he was cool.

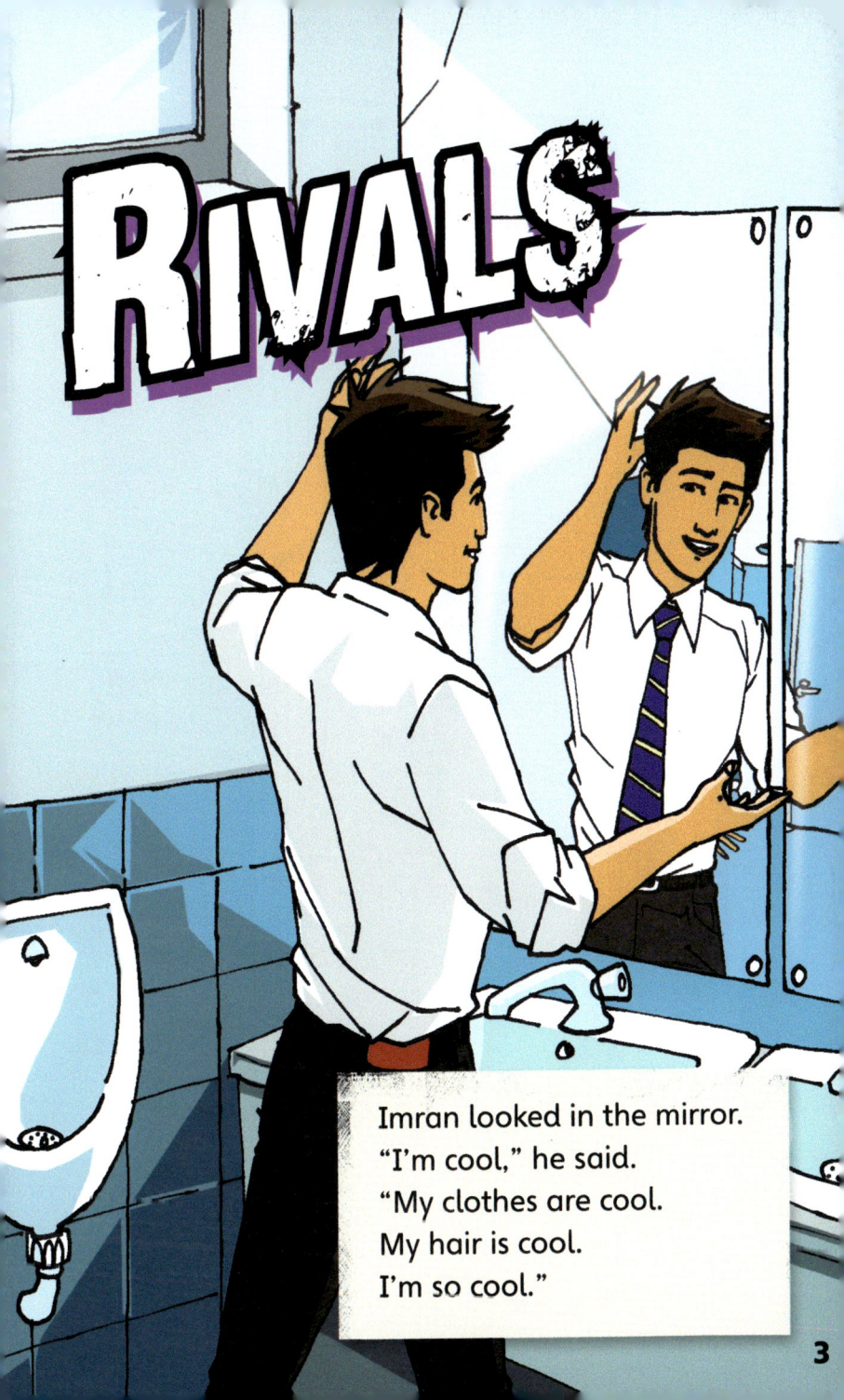

Imran looked at Tariq.
Did girls really think he was cool?

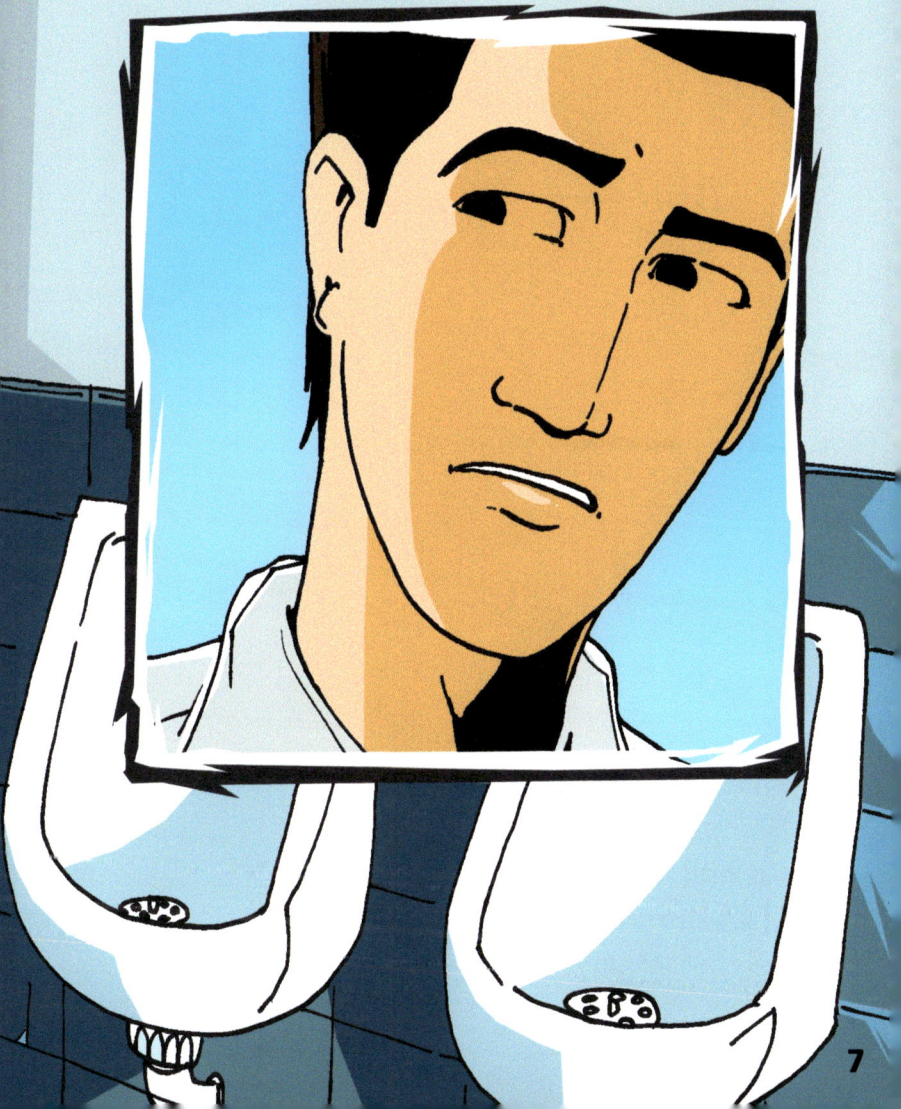

That night Imran saw Tariq at the club.
His clothes looked cool.
His hair looked cool.
Then Imran saw some girls looking at Tariq.

He went over to them.
"Do you think Tariq is cool?" he asked.
The girls looked at Tariq.
Then they looked at each other.
Then they giggled.

Tariq went over to the girls.
"Do you think Imran is cool?" he asked.
The girls looked at Imran.
Then they looked at each other.
Then they giggled a lot.

# Quiz

## Text comprehension

**Literal comprehension**
**p5** Why did Tariq laugh at Imran?
**p10** What did Tariq ask the girls?

**Inferential comprehension**
**p6** How does Tariq make Imran feel not very cool?
**p9** Why did the girls giggle when Imran asked if Tariq was cool?
**p12** How do you think the girls felt at the end?

**Personal response**
- How can you tell if someone is cool?
- Are boys more cool than girls?

## Word knowledge

**p3** Find a word that is repeated four times.
**p6** Why are the words '**You**' and '**girls**' in bold?
**p9** Find a word that means 'laughed'.

## Spelling challenge

Read these words:

**his    saw    I'm**

Now try to spell them!

## Ha! Ha! Ha!

How do bees get to school?

*By school buzz!*

# Before reading HISTORY OF COOL

## Find out about

- styles that were cool in the past like platform shoes and shell suits.

## Tricky words

- styles
- trousers
- petticoats
- pointed
- colours
- Dr Martens

*Read these words to the student. Help them with these words when they appear in the text.*

## Introduction

Some styles were cool in the past but would they be cool today? Long jackets and slim trousers were cool for guys in the 1950s and in the 1960s both guys and girls wore very bright colours. They thought those styles were cool.

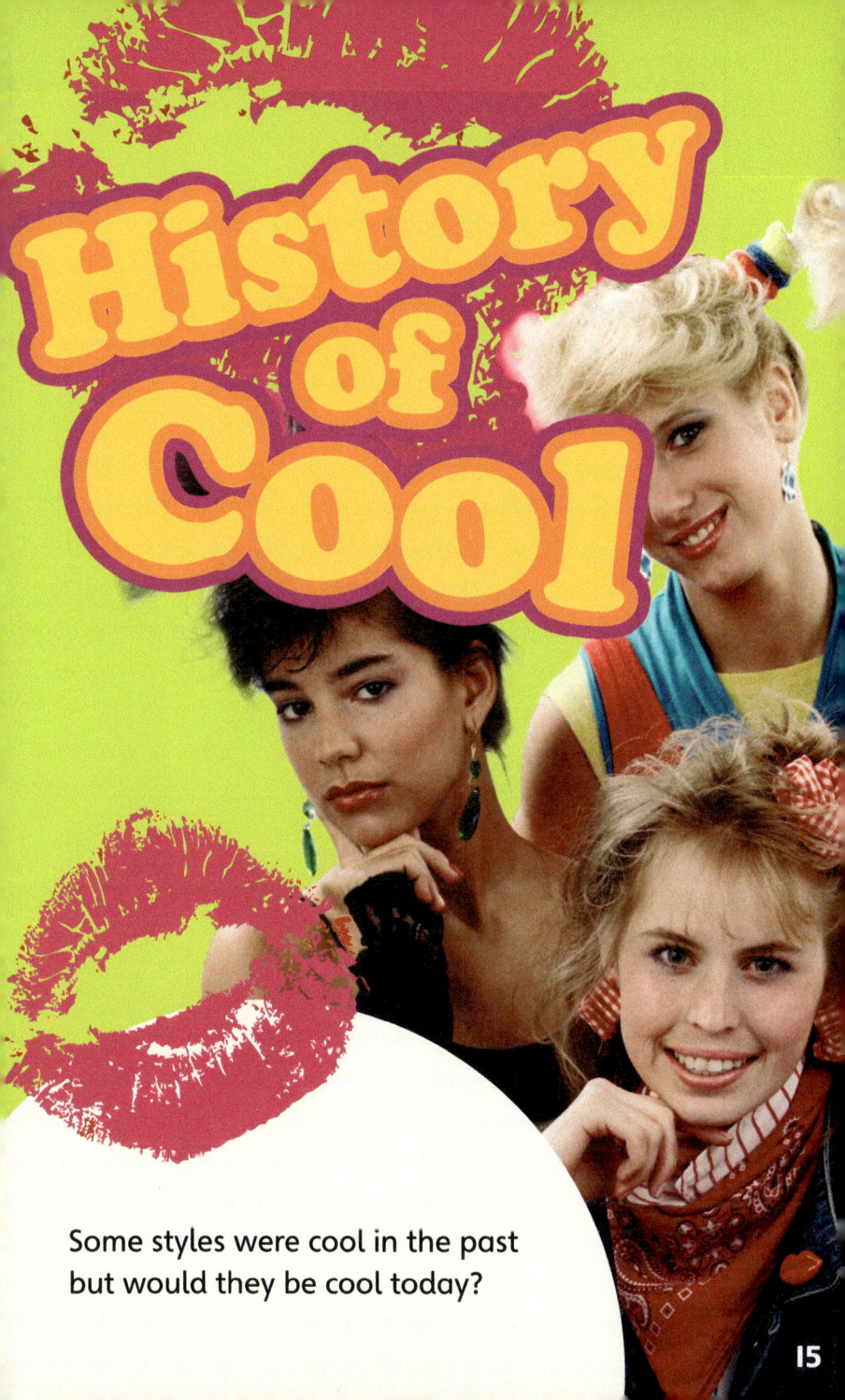

# History of Cool

Some styles were cool in the past but would they be cool today?

In the 1950s it was cool for guys to wear long jackets and slim trousers.

1950s

Girls wore lots of petticoats.

Both guys and girls wore pointed shoes. Do you think they look cool?

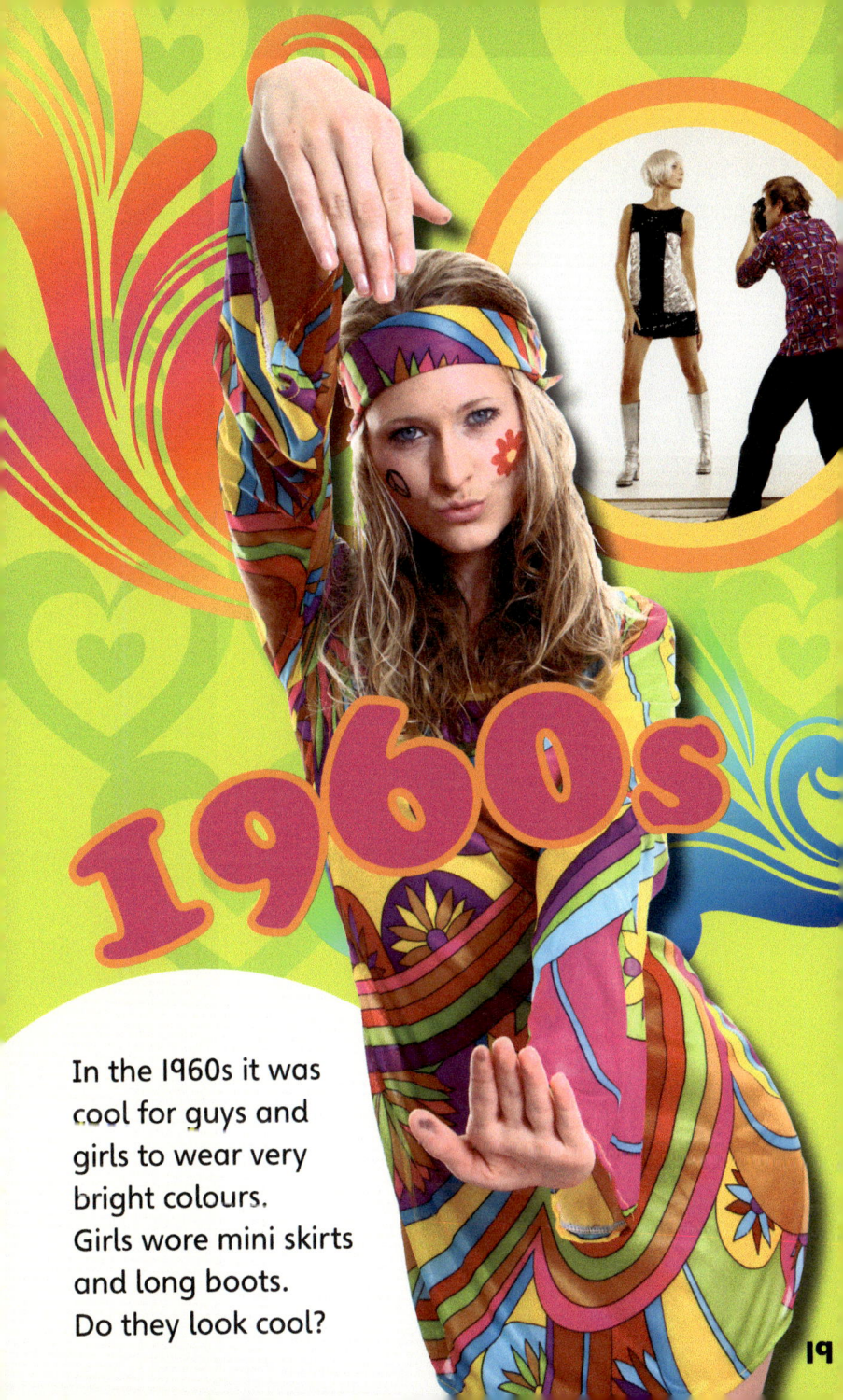

# 1960s

In the 1960s it was cool for guys and girls to wear very bright colours. Girls wore mini skirts and long boots. Do they look cool?

In the 1970s it was cool for guys to wear very wide trousers.
They wore shirts with wide ties.
Both guys and girls wore platform shoes.
Do they look cool?

1970s

# 1980s

In the 1980s it was cool for guys and girls to wear shell suits. Both guys and girls wore Dr Martens boots. Do they look cool?

# 1990s

In the 1990s it was cool for guys and girls to wear tracksuits. Both guys and girls wore trainers. Do they look cool?

# Quiz

## Text comprehension

### Literal comprehension
**p18** What did both guys and girls wear in the 1950s?
**p19** What kind of skirts did girls wear in the 1960s?

### Inferential comprehension
**p21** Why are some styles popular with guys and girls?
**p23** Why do you think fashion styles change?
**p23** Are there any styles from the past that are still stylish today?

### Personal response
- Would you wear a fashion like pointed shoes even if they were not comfortable?
- Which style of clothes from the past would you like to wear?

## Word knowledge

**p16** Find a word meaning the opposite of 'wide'.
**p18** Which adjective describes the shoes?
**p22** Find a word made of two words.

## Spelling challenge

Read these words: **the** **of** **was**
Now try to spell them!

## Ha! Ha! Ha!

What did the scarf say to the hat?

*You go on ahead, I'll hang around!*

Which clothes from the past do you think were cool?
Which styles would you wear today?
How cool are you?